WHAT'S LURKING IN THIS HOUSE?

In This Bathroom

Nancy Harris

Raintree

Chicago, Illinois

www.heinemannraintree.com
Visit our website to find out
more information about
Heinemann-Raintree books.

To order:

☎ Phone 888-454-2279

💻 Visit www.heinemannraintree.com
to browse our catalog and order online.

2010 Raintree Library
an imprint of Capstone Global Library, LLC
Chicago, Illinois

Edited by Rebecca Rissman, Nancy Dickmann,
and Sian Smith
Designed by Joanna Hinton-Malivoire
Original illustrations © Capstone Global Library LLC, 2010
Illustrated by Kevin Rechin
Picture research by Tracy Cummins
Originated by Capstone Global Library Ltd
Printed and bound in China by Leo Paper
Products Ltd

14 13 12 11 10
10 9 8 7 6 5 4 3 2 1

**Library of Congress Cataloging-in-
Publication Data**
Harris, Nancy, 1956-
In this bathroom / Nancy Harris.
  p. cm. -- (What's lurking in this house?)
  Includes bibliographical references and index.
  ISBN 978-1-4109-3724-7 (hc)
  ISBN 978-1-4109-3730-8 (pb)
1. Household pests--Juvenile literature. 2. Bacteria--
Juvenile literature. 3. Molds (Fungi)--Juvenile literature. 4.
Bathrooms--Cleaning--Juvenile literature. I. Title.
TX325.H273 2010
643'.52--dc22

2009022159

Acknowledgments
The author and publisher are grateful to the following for
permission to reproduce copyright material: Alamy pp.**18**
(© Richard Ryland); Getty Images pp.**26 bottom** (Frank
Greenaway), **28** (Barry Austin Photography); istockphoto
pp.**8** (Oleg Prikhodko), **16** (Clayton Cole), **17** (© Shaun
Lowe), **26 top** (© James Richey); Photo Researchers, Inc.
pp.**9**, **13** (© Scimat), **14** (© Steve Gschmeissner), **11** (©
Dr. Jeremy Burgess), **21** (© Edward Lettau), **23** (© Scott
Camazine), **25** (© Eye of Science); Photolibrary pp.**10** (A
Chederros), **12** (Sean Justice); Shutterstock p.**15** (©
stocksnapp); Visuals Unlimited, Inc. p.**7** (© Dr. Dennis
Kunke).

Cover photograph of a house centipede reproduced with
permission of Alamy (© Todd Bannor).

Every effort has been made to contact copyright holders
of any material reproduced in this book. Any omissions
will be rectified in subsequent printings if notice is given
to the publisher.

Some words are shown in bold, **like this.** You can find
out what they mean by looking in the glossary.

Contents

Is Something Lurking in This House?

A house is a place where you eat, sleep, work, and play. The bathroom is where you can go to get clean or use the toilet. But do you know what might be living in your bathroom?

5

How Clean Are You?

You go into the bathroom and turn on the faucet. You get in the tub and wash off. You get out and feel squeaky clean. But how can you be clean if your bathroom is full of living things called **germs**?

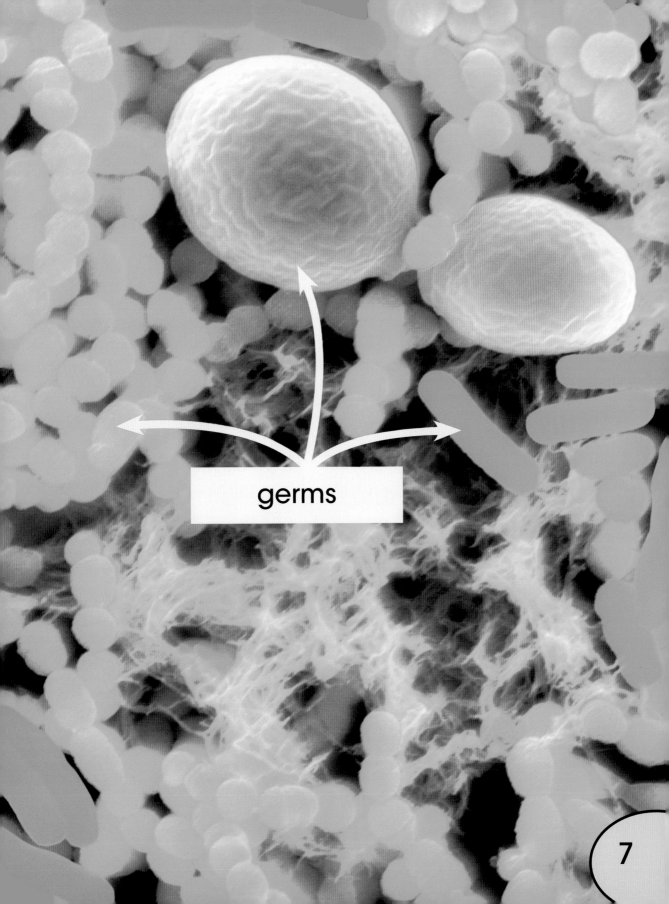
germs

Dangerous Germs

Germs are very small living things. You need to look at them through a **microscope** to see them. There are many types of germs. Germs can make you sick.

FUN FACT

Germs don't just live on the things in your bathroom. They can live on you, too!

microscope

Don't let the pretty colors of these germs fool you. They can cause some nasty illnesses.

Snacking on Skin

Bacteria are a type of **germ**. Bacteria eat the dead parts of plants and animals. Little bits of dead skin drop off of us every day. Bacteria like to eat the dead skin pieces.

More dead skin comes off when you dry yourself with a towel. This gives bacteria plenty to munch on.

Dead skin seen through a microscope.

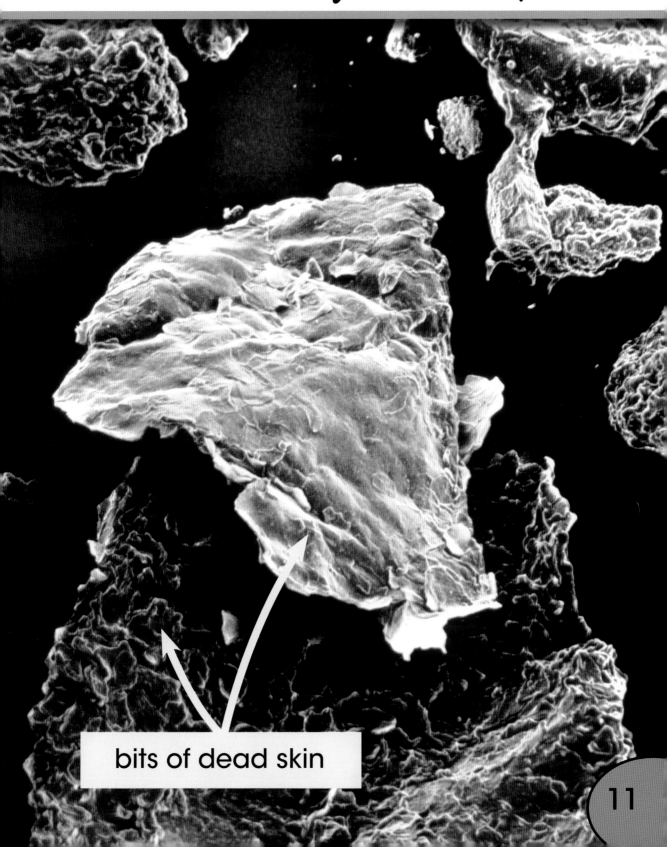

bits of dead skin

Getting Sick

Bacteria grow in your toilet bowl and on the toilet handle. They can fly out of your toilet as the dirty water is being flushed down.

Always wash your hands after you have used the bathroom. This stops **germs** from getting into your body and making you sick.

Poo is full of dangerous bacteria that can make you very ill. This is what bacteria on poo looks like under a **microscope**.

bacteria

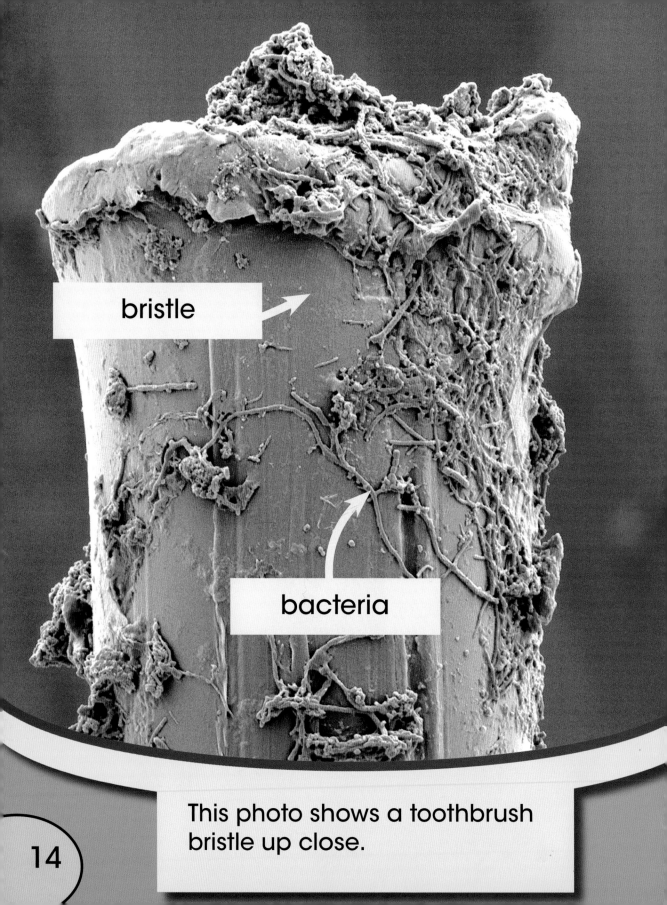

bristle

bacteria

This photo shows a toothbrush bristle up close.

Bacteria also grow on your toothbrush! You could get sore gums from the bacteria. The good news is that you can easily take care of this. Get a new toothbrush every three months!

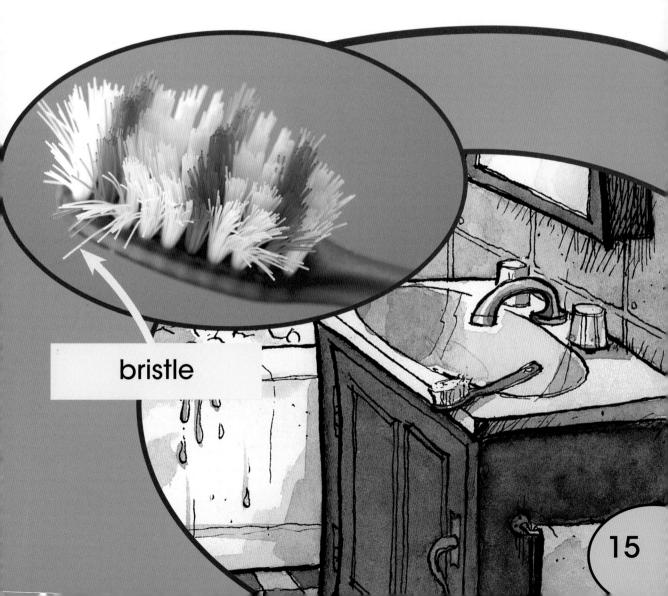

bristle

Masses of Mold

Mold is a small living thing. Mold likes to live in warm, wet places. It is easy to see why mold likes to live in the bathroom!

mold

FUN FACT

Mold can be green, blue, or yellow. It can also be white, gray, or black.

17

Would you go in a shower full of black mold?

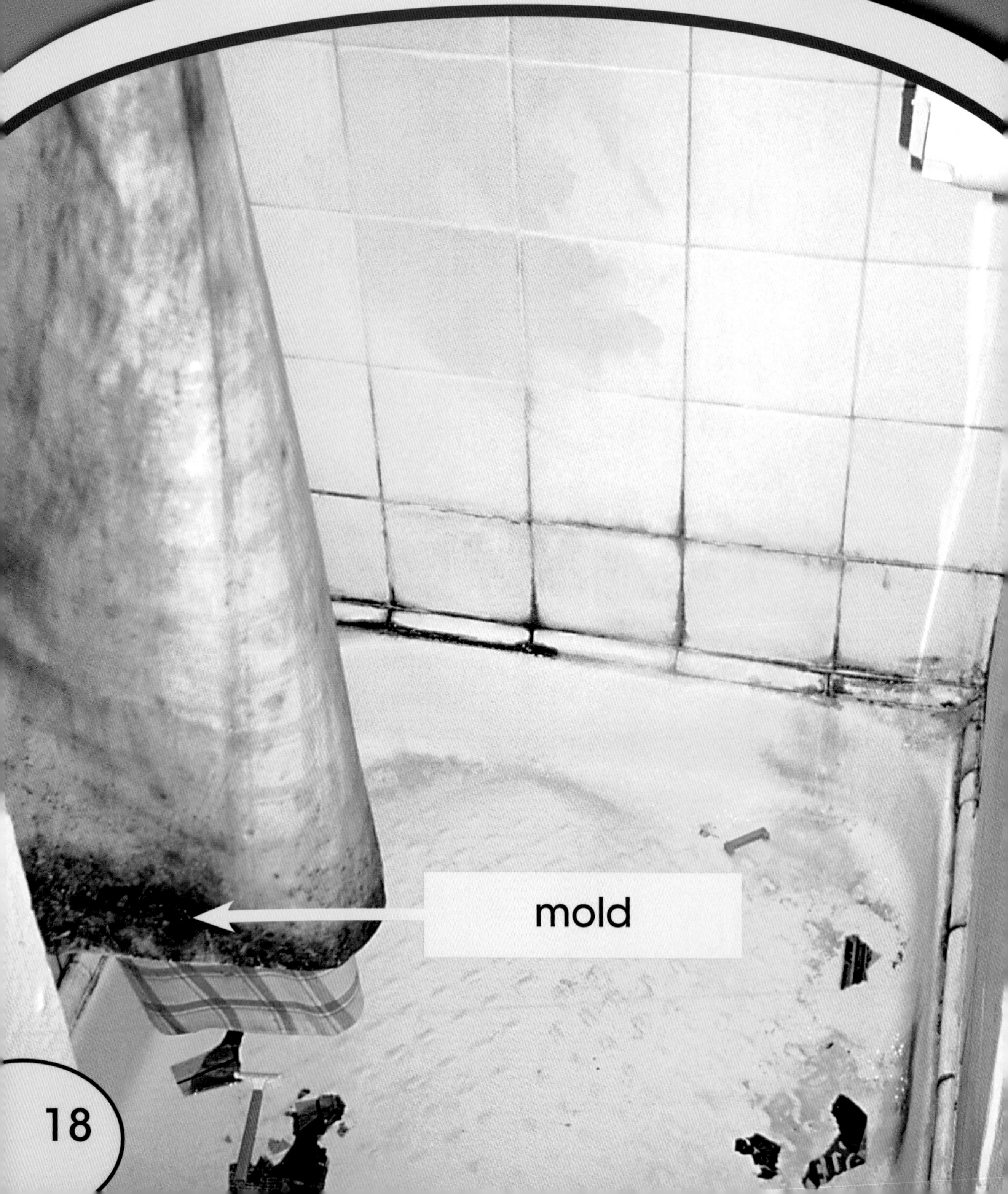

Mold can grow in many places.
It grows on floors and wallpaper.
It grows on tiles and carpet. It can
grow behind your shower wall and
all over your shower curtain.

Is Mold Harmful?

Mold can make you sick. Some people are **allergic** to mold. It makes them sneeze and cough. It can make it hard for them to breathe.

Creepy Crawly Creatures

Many types of creatures can lurk in your bathroom. House centipedes may live in the bathroom. They eat insects. They usually eat at night while you are sleeping.

FUN FACT

House centipedes have 15 pairs of legs. Imagine how fast they can move!

centipede

legs

23

Silverfish are insects that may live in your bathroom. They are silver or brown in color. They are **nocturnal**. Silverfish come out at night to eat.

FUN FACT

Silverfish eat paste, wallpaper, and mold.

silverfish

This photo shows a silverfish up close.

House centipedes will sometimes bite people. Silverfish do not. Which creature would you rather find lurking in your bathroom?

house centipede

silverfish

FUN FACT

House centipedes will eat silverfish and other pests.

Keeping It Clean

It is important to keep the bathroom clean. Use a special cleaner that kills **germs**. This will help to control the **bacteria**, mold, and creatures in the bathroom.

Fun Facts

Silverfish can survive for a year or more without food.

Wash your hands for the same length of time as it takes to say the alphabet. This will get them clean.

"Centipede" means "one hundred feet." House centipedes only have 15 pairs of feet. Some other types of centipede have more than 100 feet!

If one of a house centipede's legs is held down, the centipede can drop that leg off. The centipede can then escape while its attacker is busy looking at the twitching leg!

Glossary

allergic when you are allergic to something, your body reacts badly to it. For example, some people are allergic to mold; it makes them sneeze.

bacteria tiny living things. Bacteria are a type of germ.

germs tiny living things that can make you ill if they get inside your body

microscope instrument used to see very small things such as germs

nocturnal describes animals that sleep during the daytime and come out at night

Find Out More

Books

Hall, Margaret. *Centipedes.*
  Mankato, MN: Capstone, 2006.

Ridley, Sarah. *Where to Find Minibeasts:*
  Minibeasts in the Home. Mankato, MN:
  Smart Apple Media, 2009.

Taylor-Butler, Christine. *Tiny Life in the Air.*
  Danbury, CT: Children's Press, 2005.

Websites

http://kidshealth.org/kid/talk/qa/germs.html
This section on the Kid's Health Website tells
you about germs and how to protect yourself
from them.

http://www.kids-science-experiments.com/
growingmold.html
This Website contains a science experiment on
how to grow mold.

Find out

What do good
bacteria in our
bodies do?

Index